Dawson goes to Yellowstone

Copyright © 2019 by Waldo W. Montgomery, Jr.

Waldo W. Montgomery, Jr.
200 Lake Road, Apt 904
Belton, TX 76513
wwmontgom@outlook.com

First Edition

ISBN 978-0-9823643-3-8

Text by Waldo W. Montgomery, Jr.

Photographs by Waldo W. Montgomery, Jr.

To my Facebook friends and my feline pals Bogey and Tidbit

Hi, Everyone! My name is Dawson. I'm an American Eskimo—that's a dog breed in case you didn't know. My human dad's name is Waldo. Don't laugh! I know what you're thinking—"Where's Waldo?" Right? Well I can tell you where he is much of the time—Yellowstone National Park! I know because he takes me with him. Like Dad, I love going to Yellowstone, and I don't mind the long three-day drive from Texas to the park—it's worth it. We make the trip twice a year in the spring and fall. Dad calls it a pilgrimage. He tells our friends and neighbors back home that he hears the wolves calling, and that's the reason we go to Yellowstone so often. They think he's joking, but I know better. Wolves are his favorite park animals.

But my favorite park animals are ground squirrels! I always look for them when we take walks at pullouts and parking lots.

My favorite park animal

The park rules say that because I'm a dog, I must always be on a leash, and I can't be more than one hundred feet from a road or parking lot. That's for my safety. Wolves, bears, coyotes, bison, and moose don't like dogs. Some park animals are territorial and dangerous, so we always must be aware of the risk they pose and keep a respectful distance from them.

When we drive through the park, I enjoy hanging out the car window and watching for wildlife. They are both interesting and fascinating. I'm always courteous and never bark or growl at them. I know Yellowstone is their home and I'm a guest, so it's important I be on my best behavior.

Dad and I usually stay in Gardiner, Montana, at the park's north entrance. Sometimes we discover elk grazing right outside our door! Elk can be dangerous so we don't get too close to them, and we never feed them.

There are also a lot of small mule deer in town. They seem curious about everything—especially me. One of them, I think, had a crush on me and followed me when Dad took me for walks. I tried to ignore her, but she wouldn't go away! She was definitely not my type!

For the past four years, we have visited Yellowstone in May hoping to see wolf pups when they emerge from their den. Dad says that to see Yellowstone's wolves and their pups, park visitors must be on their schedule. For us, that means our day begins at 3AM! That's my job—I always make sure Dad is up. After he dresses and puts my winter sweater on, we go for a walk. After eating a quick breakfast, Dad loads the car with everything we need for the day. I immediately snuggle down in my warm bed in the backseat. We leave Gardiner at 4:30 A.M. and usually arrive at the wolves' den area by 5:30, which is first light. It's also cold at that hour. I don't "do" cold mornings!

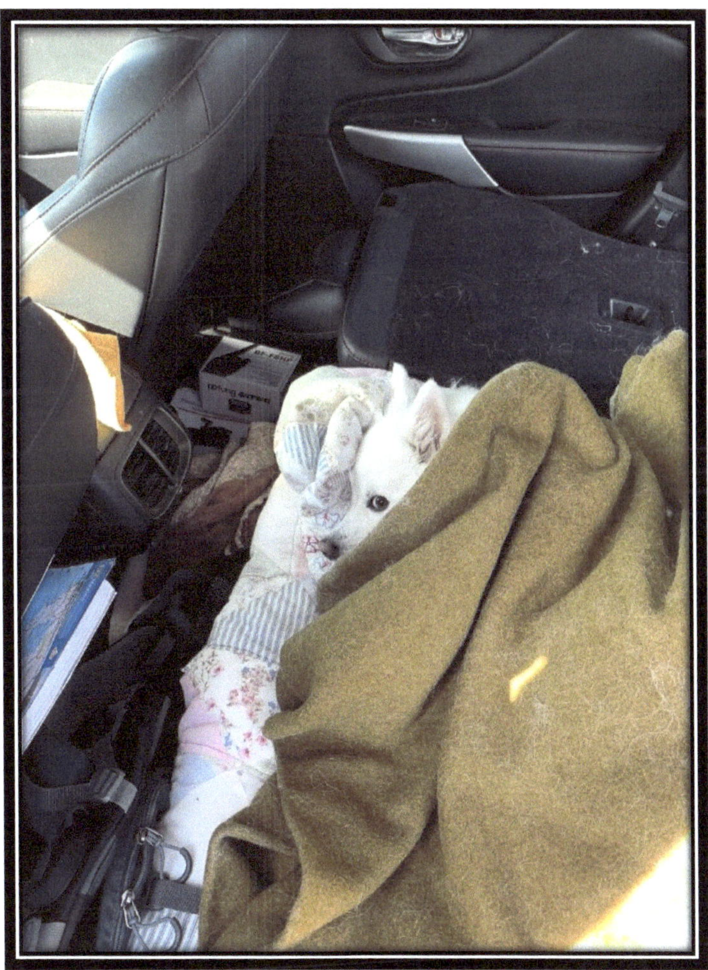

I'm content to stay under my blanket until it warms up.

Dad, on the other hand, loves the cold, especially if the wolves are out and about. I'm happy for him. He's in wolf heaven and doesn't mind that I prefer sleeping in the car.

My dad, "The Wolf Man"

When it warms up, I help Dad look for wolves and other wildlife, especially ground squirrels. Slough Creek is one of our favorite places.

Wolf watching is exhausting work.

A pronghorn antelope pauses to check me out.

You might think most people would have better things to do, like maybe sleeping, instead of getting up in the wee hours and racing off to the park in the dark hoping to see wolves. But you would be surprised how many wolf watchers there are in the park at first light. I was amazed the first time I saw them—then I crawled under my blanket in the backseat.

As you can see, I'm not out there in the cold and rain with all those wolf and bear watchers; that's because my Mama didn't raise any dumb pups!

Around mid-morning, when it's a civilized hour and a lot warmer, Dad usually succeeds in persuading me to get out of the car and socialize a bit. I notice right away how excited Dad and the other wolf watchers become when they suddenly hear a pack of wolves howling on a distant ridge. "That's music to my ears!" one of them exclaims as he peers at them through his spotting scope. Some of the women even have tears in their eyes! Well, yeah, those wolves are pretty impressive standing together on that snow-covered ridge howling their beautiful song. I even feel compelled to join in!

So I do. The nearest wolf watchers fall silent and look at me with a mixture of amusement and disbelief. Dad grins as he snaps a photo of me, then says to the other wolf watchers, "Now *that's* music to my ears!" Meanwhile, the wolves on the ridge continue to howl. Maybe they hear me; maybe not. Regardless, I can howl with the best of them! Just sayin'!

Dad and I have an understanding: The cold mornings are his to spend looking for wolves, and the warm afternoons are mine to spend exploring the park, whiffing and sniffing, and seeing other wildlife. We usually eat lunch at one of two favorite places. The first is in Little America Valley which the wolf watchers call "Boulders." We sit on a big rock that Dad has named "Dawson's Rock" and enjoy the beautiful scenery while we eat lunch. Dad always packs a slice of turkey or a turkey hot dog for me.

Another favorite lunch spot is Round Prairie in the Lamar Valley. As the name implies, it's a small prairie through which flows a pretty stream, and it's surrounded by spectacular snow-capped mountains. Round Prairie makes a beautiful picture any time of the year.

After lunch, we spend the afternoon looking for wildlife and places for me to explore. I'm always on high alert as we drive through the park! We never know what surprises wait for us around the next bend! Bison are everywhere. They are also very dangerous, so we always give them a lot of room. Unfortunately, a few park visitors are injured every year by bison because they don't remember to keep a respectful distance from them. We never know when one, or sometimes a whole herd, will step out into the road and block traffic. These are called "critter jams," and sometimes they can be pretty scary. Sometimes, too, a herd of bison will walk down the middle of the road. That's because it's the easiest way for them to get from one place to another, especially in winter when the snow is deep. When "critter jams" occur, we just have to be patient and wait until they decide to move aside or get off the road. After all, it *is* their park!

"Theres a critter jam up ahead, Dad!"

And "critter jams" can be pretty scary at times...

...really scary! These bison don't look very friendly!

I think coyotes are cool and fun to watch. We often see them in the Lamar Valley hunting for voles which are small rodents. Unlike Texas coyotes, those in Yellowstone show little fear of park visitors. Dad enjoys videoing and photographing them, especially family groups consisting of Mom and Dad and their pups. Sometimes when I'm hanging out the car window, we will see them near the road. Occasionally they will stop and stare at me.

I think this coyote wanted to invite me for lunch! No thanks!

Bears are the most popular park animal. Dad and I always watch for them. Very often we see black bears alongside the road. However, I never bark or growl. We don't want to disturb them.

One morning while driving to the Lamar Valley, Dad spotted a grizzly at the Blacktail Ponds and stopped at the base of a slope to photograph it. He jumped out of the car and opened the rear cargo door to get his tripod. In his excitement, he forgot to close it. He then trudged up the slope and set up his camera and tripod. He didn't tell me I couldn't come—so I did. Dad wasn't happy when he glanced down and saw me sitting at his feet. "Go place," he said, pointing at the car. I did as I was told and ran down the slope and jumped into the back of the car. I stayed there until Dad returned a minute or two later. He was a bit shaken and angry at himself. I think it was over his carelessness in not closing the cargo door. "That could have been bad," he said, giving me a hug. "Thanks for obeying me. I won't make that mistake again." Meanwhile, the grizzly went about his business, seemingly unaware of us.

While black bears and grizzly bears are interesting, they are also a bit scary. I prefer watching wildlife more my size or smaller.

River otters, like these, are especially entertaining. But that water sure looks cold!

Cute little critters called voles are among my favorites, although they're not as large or easy to spot as ground squirrels.

Among Dad's best-loved wolves are these two Junction Butte Pack yearlings. I like them, too. They're pretty cool. The one in the first picture below we call "Raven." He got the name because he was often seen in the company of ravens. Raven also appears in the second photo standing to the left of his beautiful sister whom we call "Gypsy." Gypsy got her name because she was often seen wandering alone in the park.

On one of our recent trips to Yellowstone, Dad and I stayed at Stop the Car Trading Post in Silver Gate, Montana. It's only a mile from the park's northeast entrance. Dad especially liked it because the cabin part of the Trading Post is called "The Wolf Den!" We enjoyed our time there. It was rustic, extremely comfortable, and just a short drive from Yellowstone's famous Lamar Valley with its bountiful wildlife.

Late one night I woke Dad up. I was just a bit scared. Maybe it was because there were wolves howling right outside our bedroom wall! Together, we just lay in bed and listened to them. It so happened that it was also Dad's birthday. He thought it was the best birthday present ever! Later that morning we went outside the cabin and found wolf tracks just three feet from where we were sleeping!

Dad and I stayed here during our fall 2018 trip. Loved it!

The Wolf Den had everything we could want, including wolves howling outside our bedroom wall! We even found wolf tracks!

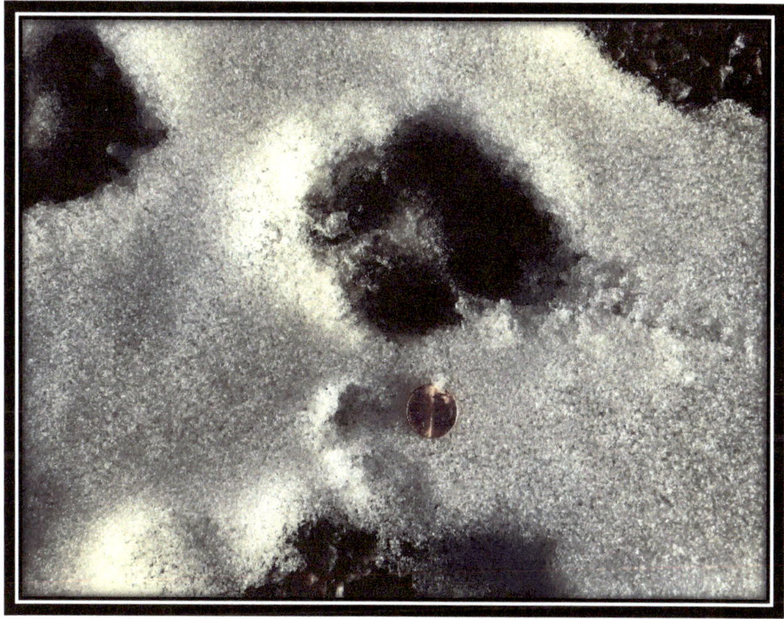

I'm always dazzled by the park's seasonal beauty.

And what makes our trips to Yellowstone extra special is when Mom comes too!

I hope, my friend, you have enjoyed my Yellowstone adventures. Maybe we'll meet in the park one day. I would like that! Until then, I'll share with you one thing I have learned from my many trips to the park:

YELLOWSTONE NEVER DISAPPOINTS!

Dawson

And my sidekick, Waldo